The Magical Breasts
of Britney Spears

The Magical Breasts

of Britney Spears

RYAN G. VAN CLEAVE

 RED HEN PRESS | *Los Angeles, California*

The Magical Breasts of Britney Spears

Cover Design by Mark E. Cull

ISBN: 1-59709-067-0

Library of Congress Catalog Card Number: 2006921407

Published by Red Hen Press

The City of Los Angeles Cultural Affairs Department, California Arts Council, Los Angeles County Arts Commission and National Endowment for the Arts partially support Red Hen Press.

First edition

Acknowledgments

Grateful acknowledgment is made to the following publications in which the poems, sometimes in slightly different versions, appeared: *Barrow Street, The Chaffin Journal, Cider Press Review, Clackamas Literary Review, descant, Diagram, Diner, Eclipse, Fire (U.K.), Floating Holiday, Grand Street, Harpur Palate, The Homestead Review, Lullwater Review, Maize, Ontario Review, Oregon East, RE:AL, River Oak Review, Southern Humanities Review, Third Coast.*

Some of these poems, collected as *Bubbles Speaks*, received second prize in the 2005 *Main Street Rag* Poetry Chapbook Contest.

"Mr. Bertel Poem #3, or Smart-ass-ology 101" received Honorable Mention in the 2004 *Harpur Palate* Milton Kessler Poetry Award.

"Music Theory as Chaos.com, or the Magical Breasts of Britney Spears" received Honorable Mention in the 2002 Willamette Award in Poetry from *Clackamas Literary Review.*

"I ♥ Tiger Woods" won second prize in the 2002 *Diner* Poetry Contest.

"Blue Man Group & the Shiftiness of *Wu Wei*" won the 2002 *Harpur Palate* Milton Kessler Poetry Award and was also honored in the 2001 *Glimmer Train* Poetry Contest.

I thank the following writers and poets for their ongoing support and inspiration: Peter Meinke, Martín Espada, Stephen Dunn, Rachel Loden, Vivian Shipley, and the late A. R. Ammons, not necessarily in this order. My special thanks go to Miles Garett Watson for his generous and sensitive help with this and other projects. Special appreciation also goes to my wife, Victoria, for her blind faith, indefatigable support, and "1st grader sense of humor."

CONTENTS

You both smoke, you both drink,
and you both cheated on significant others after three years.
You guys are made for each other.

> – Shar Jackson, upon hearing of the Britney Spears/Kevin
> Federline engagement while Shar was pregnant with Kevin's
> second child

As we arrive, I turn and look out the door,
People are greeting us right at the shore.

A meal, a shower and some ice cream
Then I threw my man down, you know what I mean!

> – from Britney Spears' "A Honeymoon Poem"

Who Wants to Be a Millionaire

Music Theory as Chaos.com,
or the Magical Breasts of Britney Spears

Music Lesson Numero Uno (as told by my first-ever guitar teacher,
        Scott, whose self-proclaimed nickname was "The Party Train"):
If you fuck up a note, do it again and again like you meant it. That's jazz.
        I've kept this thought over the years of trying to teach Whitman
to a pack of beaky, cheeky geeks who can't understand that their
        trajectory in the universe is one of their own making, fueled
not by sugary gimmicks or cool turtle-bone shades, but curiosity,
        the type of self-challenge that comes from asking: Why did God
let us cover the 70s in faux fur, glorious shag? And why hasn't some
        genius created a 24-hour Adult Video Store & Deli?

So when I squawked a wrong note in the middle of an explanation
        on Whitman and the social responsibility of the poet (the crux
of this boo-boo was a claim that the Parthenon was built in Rome – don't ask),
        the girl with soft vowels, monosyllabic clothes, the one
who waits her whole life for moments like these – you know her –
        stands up in all her bosomless glory, announcing, *The Parthenon,*
or the temple of Athene Parthenos (i.e. the maiden), was built on the Acropolis
        at Athens in mid–400 B.C. by Pericles to honor the city's patron goddess
and to commemorate the recent Greek victory over the Persians. Remembering
        The Party Train's maxim, I said, "You sure? Why don't you look

that up and report to the class next week?" which is akin to asking
        a student to watch *Gandhi* three times in a row without popcorn,
Zoloft, or Irish coffee. But the great gas cloud of a smirk on her face told me
        she was going to do it. I wanted to Ctrl+Alt+Delete the whole
thing, reboot the damn class, when another kid who hadn't so much
        as coughed restlessly all semester, let alone speak, said, *It's a little*
like the new Britney Spears album – she's "stronger than yesterday/now it's nothing
        but my way/My loneliness ain't killing me no more" to which I ask,
"What?" Another girl who I swear couldn't comprehend anything
        but a star-crossed system of dating, said, *Did you know you can email*

her? It's Britney@Britney.com, and five people jotted that down inside
        the cover of their used copies of *Leaves of Grass.* "Just hold on,"
I said, feeling a mouse-click away from Chaos.com, a website I once found
        that features random red squiggles. "What does Britney Spears have
in common with Walt Whitman, one of the real benchmark names in the
        development of a truly American literature?" A chunky C+ kid
said, *Her breasts give me vertigo.* And then it erupted. Someone else:
        She had a job, from A to C, man. Another kid: *Just like my art history
grades.* Me: *Kill me now, Lord. Quick.* And I imagined myself, the Patron Saint
        of Classroom Disasters, going Gene Simmons right there, wagging

a black tongue as I bust guitars atop their heads like a human xylophone.
        But it was Parthenon Girl who saved the day, saying, *Britney's
a perfect example of a distinctly American mentality, the poster child of hard
        bodies and soft music. She's the pop icon extension of Whitman, but also
the antithesis of him, inevitably.* We ended on the clang of that note, all
        hurrying home to ponder the elemental breakdown of an entire
class like an Alka-Seltzer in a giant glass of water. I cracked open two
        beers and flipped on the tube – there she was, Britney, hawking Pepsi
in a blue jumpsuit that covered her bosom like a liqueur dousing does
        an angel food cake. Even my dog paused mid-scratch to eyeball

the screen, the way her abracadabra breasts defied gravity as if in an
        assertion that God himself was a lighter-than-air device, and I
realized that in the glitz-bomb grip of hands such as hers, poor Walt
        Whitman didn't stand a chance, and neither, quite frankly, did I.
Later, as my thoughts thinned towards sleep, I could almost hear it,
        the torn flesh of stars opening like a mouth to say, *Oops! . . . I did it again.*

Blue Man Group & the Shiftiness of Wu Wei

I'm trying to decide if they don't speak because no one can figure out
      just what the hell blue fellows with banana-ooze spray-plugs
in their chests might have to say or whether their silence is a commentary
      on the vatic moments of our lives, how 93.6% of the words we speak
are hollow as the PVC pipe marimba they're jamming bad 80s tunes on.
      My wife starts to boogey under her plastic raincoat, jiving along
with little funky chicken hand moves, and most of the audience is, too,
      really digging this blue trio, and I catch myself firing up the "Who's
Your Daddy?" arm swing and hip shake, which really isn't about

      the experience of fatherhood, but more along the lines
of "Daddy-o" or "Sugar daddy," where the paternal character of the word
      gives way to pseudo-sexual Electra-complex overtones. Suddenly,
I'm struck with a *zzzzzzZZZZAAAPPP* of existential angst as I realize
      that the dancer both asks AND answers the same question:
"Who's your Daddy? . . . I am your Daddy," which disturbs me on eleven
      levels, so I shut my eyes and hunker into my clear poncho as
the dingbat preschool-teacher-looking woman sitting next to me (prissy,
      Payless shoes, white linen dress) says, *Do you think they're blue ALL over?*

And now I'm thinking about plugged pores and acne scars, blue latex
      gloves that choke oxygen out of your skin, how there's four Blue
Man Group teams in Chicago and they're completely interchangeable
      because as long as there's idiots in blue facepaint and jumpsuits
on stage, they'll look enough like the guys in the Pentium commercials
      to please the crowd. And as the giant toilet paper streamers descend
upon us at the end of the show, I'm still stuck on the idea of answering/
      asking, the oxymoronic quality of life, the very same beachglass-
in-the-soles-of-your-feet unignorability that steered me into philosophy

as an undergraduate, where I learned about *wu wei* and the *Tao Te Ching* which mutually define each other, this the lesson from my
philosophy of religion professor, Dr. Kissel, whose glass eye
was the color of a chestnut while the good one was, of course, Blue Man
Group blue. Dr. Kissel once said, *Wu wei is both nothing and doing, it's action-not-action,* and I remember thinking wow, zero-to-infinity
in six seconds. One time in an elevator at Reavis Hall,
home of the philosophy, sociology, American studies, economics,
linguistics, and Caribbean literature folks, Dr. Kissel, alone

in that elevator with me, punched the STOP button. Alarm bells rang
in the distance. Then he leaned close, and boozily said, *I'll tell you what philosophy is, it's a hypodermic of sea monkeys right in your skull.*
A short time after that, I was an English major, where I thought
of myself in *wu wei* terms, both as "valiant warrior" and "helpless victim."
A few weeks later, during an Internet investigation into
"Shakespeare's Use of the Semicolon as Repressed Adulterous Guilt,"
I typed *wu wei* into a search engine and found www.wuwei.com,
which gave me this message: "I'm toast and I am not functioning anymore.

I'm frozen and I can't move. I love all of you." When Blue Man
Group's neon glow-in-the-dark skeleton band kicks into the exit number,
a rock-n-roll heavy-bass riff that has the Red Briar Theater seats
beneath us shaking, I follow my wife out in a surge of bodies past
the tube-choked walls of the entryway and then into the chill
Chicago evening, where starlight has just begun to burst to life upon
an indigo evening sky. My wife grabs my hand, says, *Well, what'cha think about the show? Did you like it?* I think of silly Twinkie skits and
sledgehammer social criticism paired against how her folks

dropped fifty bucks times four tickets; I feel the downward yank of gravity
in my gut increasing as I quickly answer, *Yes-not-yes,* and my wife,
no Taoist guru, knows exactly what I mean.

Counter-Terrorist Barbie

She handles an M-16 assault rifle as easily
as her cousin, Short-Order Barbie, slings hash
at the rib joint over on 17th Avenue.

But seeing Muslim fanatics and Hannibal
Lecter carnivores in every urban shadow comes at
its price – under CT Barbie's pillow, a phosphorous

grenade and loaded Beretta pistol. She's
a crack shot at 300 yards, can put out the eye
of a blue jay even in a stiff wind. Tonight, though,

she lies facedown atop a thirty-two story building,
infrared binoculars in hand, watching for *El Guerrero
Cobre* to arrive at the UN safehouse with his radio-

triggered explosives, the necklace of human ears
a mere bulge under his shirt. An evening sheen of sweat
covers CT Barbie, and she rolls a 7.72mm bullet

between her fingers like an old lover once explored
her tongue stud. As the young Uruguayan bomber lurks
onto the scene, she settles crosshairs onto his forehead

and thinks of angels massing overhead, the Mozart
concierto she once knew on cello, her middle-class
parents who believer she's an FBI bookkeeper –

so damn proud of her, so proud their baby done good.

Marilyn in the House of Mirrors

Take these treasures, earth, now that no one living can enjoy them.
– Beowulf

It's easy to lose true north
in the blueback wonder
of so many shiny oceans,
every shore pocked with empty
shells, pink-eared mollusks,
seaweed curlicues, thick chunks
of glass that reflect Ursula
Majora and a skyful of bright.
Marilyn shuts her eyes, wakes
up complaining just like the rest
of us, her limbs numb, the slow
drag of wood dozing into sand.
As a child, her father startled
her with certain words: *sagebrush,*
solitary, Sister Immaculata. As she lay
panting for breath before a blank
mirror, she lunged at it, pointing
out the brushstrokes that whited
her from view. But try angle after
angle – like strangers mishearing
every cry for help – she remained
alone, guideless, the last few hours
an uneventful séance filled with
quiet, and the dull chuntering of birds.

Trivia Gone Wrong, or How I Didn't Win Ben Stein's Money

"Pumpernickel" in German means "devil's fart." It's illegal to own
  a red car in Shanghai, China. The most shoplifted book
  in the United States is the Bible. These are the facts I know,
the kernels of truth that hum like wasps nesting in my head.
  I blame my mother who, when I was five, poured me a glass
of lemonade and said, *Did you know armadillos can get leprosy?*

I was hooked. The more useless these random tidbits, the tastier.
  Like "tsunamis travel as fast as jet planes." Or "on some
  Caribbean islands, the oysters can climb trees." My father's
to blame too, a jokester who on several occasions at family
  dinner parties confessed, *I had amnesia once. Or twice.*
So it's no surprise that when the Ben Stein folks scoured Chicago

for "eager, knowledgeable contestants with a penchant for trivia,"
  I went, dredging up twenty years of crap from the darkest
  recesses of my mind. Most polar bears are left-handed.
It takes six months to build a Rolls Royce, thirteen hours for a Camry.
  During a romantic evening of snow crab legs and some rather
flat soda, I told my then-girlfriend that Diet Pepsi was originally called

"Patio Diet Cola." Her response: "You should skip marriage and jump
  right ahead to divorce." I later bought her a bumper sticker that
  said, "Jesus is coming – everyone look busy." She wasn't amused.
Anyway, I got to the fake studio setup at the Hyatt and though my buzzer
  malfunctioned twice, I knew who said, "I think the sexiest thing
a woman can do is be as fat as me, or fatter" (Roseanne Arnold) as well as

that the g in "g-string" stands for "groin." No biggies, maybe,
        but enough to fly me out to L.A. for the real deal two months
        later. The beehive-haired stewardess for Delta kept asking me
if I wanted anything – a first class freebie, after all – but I was too engrossed
        in a list I'd been making of possible questions and answers.
"Uh-oh" in Swahili is "Wee!" and "Eeny-meeny-miny-mo" in Italian

is "Ambaraba chichicoco." McDonald's sells "McSpaghetti"
        in the Philippines and "McLak" salmon burgers in Norway.
        None of the original Beatles knew how to read music, though
it's a trick question, sort of, because Paul McCartney eventually taught
        himself years later. Well, I met Ben Stein backstage before
the show – he shook my hand, then eyed me and the other two

contestants, saying in a way-over-the-top Arkansas accent, "Y'all don't
        look any smarter than Texas termites," which put the Chi Omega
        blonde on my left into tears, blubbering, "I can't **believe** I let
my boyfriend talk me into this." The buzzcut guy with a green Detroit U.
        t-shirt and torn jeans said under his breath, "Her belt doesn't
go through all the loops," which made Ben's producer hurry out

with tissues for the girl, a copy of the consent forms for the guy (we
        promised to be on our best behavior), and a bottle of sparkling
        water for me because I looked "a bit like my chimney might
be clogged." Sure enough, that kind-hearted intern did me in. My eyes
        glazed, the show started, and the answers were like Mackinac
peaches – always out of season. I said "Montana" instead of

"Minnesota." I said Thomas Jefferson created the phonograph
        instead of Thomas Edison, though I later told Ben that
        "When Edison played 'Mary Had a Little Lamb' on his
first crude recording device in 1877, he was really trying to create
        an answering machine because unlike the telegraph,
the telephone didn't take messages. The Wizard of Menlo Park

gave up on that, though." After telling Ben this when the show
        was long over – and yes, that damn Chi Omega went home
        sobbing with five grand in her green leather Gucci purse –
Ben just shook his head, then took out his wallet and handed me
        a crisp ten-dollar bill. "Please, just take this and go," he said,
waving to the bull-necked security guys who hoisted me out like

a sack of potatoes. Still, my folks saw their kid on the tube, and I got
        a 5-CD changer as a wonderful parting gift, but sometimes
        I think, if only they'd asked, "Which are bigger? An ostrich's
eyes or its brains?" (Eyes) or "Which month has the most fatal
        auto accidents?" (July) That moment of potential game show
glory was an upstart weed I trampled all to hell – it's irony, I know,

much like Ramses condoms, which are named after Ramses II,
        an Egyptian pharaoh who fathered 160+ children, or that
        in Waterloo, Napoleon was bedridden with hemorrhoids.
I still think about *Jeopardy!* and *Who Wants to Be a Millionaire*
        but I don't try out. Just knowing that the U.S. government spent
$277,000 on pickle research in 1977 is its own pleasure and reward.

I ♥ Tiger Woods

No one travels the dark arteries of obsession on purpose – we forget
    this sometimes upon seeing the ugly purplish underbelly:
        celebrity stalking, photo/memorabilia shrines, tattoos,
    Fed-Exing your cuticles and hair snippings. When my girlfriend
        of two years told me as we eased between the coffee-

colored banks of the Apalachicola River in a rented-by-the-hour canoe
    that she loved "that beautiful man, who looks like a pencil
        sketching of God," I didn't expect the worst. After all,
    we had the Okey-Dokey List, which the makers of *Friends*
        later ripped off, a Five-Famous-Folks-My-Significant-

Other-Gives-The-Okey-Dokey-To-Sleep-With-No-Guilt-No-Strings-
    Attached List, and I had five doozies myself: Julia Roberts (later
        she gets bumped for Britney Va-va-va-voom Spears),
    Heather Locklear (God bless hot pink bikinis and unpinned hair),
        Janet Jackson (can't explain this one, other than this vague

equation – me, a well-weathered flintlock + her, a powderbag = ka-BLAM!)
    and two others who've since been replaced so many times
        I can't hazard a guess who they might've been then,
    though in the sloshing subsoil of memory, I suspect Madonna
        and her gold-coned breasts may have been in the mix.

On a fishing trip to Lake Lucerne years ago, a Methodist forest preserve
    in Wisconsin, my father took me boating at dusk on the lake; not
        five minutes out into the roiling reed-patches, I saw
    a little snapper turtle the color of sumac leaves, red like a fireball.
        I stretched too far, dumped us both face-first into murky

black water. Later, he told me, "You can't always get what you want,"
    and I tried to explain that I didn't want the turtle, not in a bag-
        him-up-take-him-home-keep-him-in-a-plastic-fishbowl-
    until-he-starves-himself-to-death sort of way, but rather I just
        wanted to press my fingers to the shell, touch his brimstone

belly, let his silver eyes fall upon me in a moment Thoreau would've envied.
    But I couldn't explain it right then, and Tabitha, my Tiger-loving
        woman, must've felt the same way with me because after she
    bought her ninth pair of "I ♥ Tiger" underwear, I began to ask
        questions. Then came the clippings, hundreds from *Golf*

Digest, *Sports Illustrated*, *TV Guide*, everywhere, and she pasted them
    to the ceiling of our bedroom, the front door, over the stove,
        even atop the toilet lid. By now, Tiger had won
    the Masters and was being hailed as one of the three greatest
        golfers of all time already. Then came the tattoo, bright

orange block letters, right above her bellybutton: *This is Tiger country*.
    A week later, she and two other Tigerettes – as they dubbed
        themselves – went "on tour" like Deadheads with their #1 band
    or folks did with The Beatles in the 60s. I told my friends and family
        she was trying to kick a Percocet habit in rehab.

Time groaned past slowly, softly, like a thrush waiting outside
    a windowpane, and I never saw Tabitha again, but imagine
        my surprise when, two years to the day later, a hot pink
    "I ♥ Tiger" pennant appears dead-center on my lawn like the flag
        marking the sixteenth hole at Pebble Creek. I yanked it

from the ground, feeling something descending Icarus-like from the sky,
    and no one was around screaming "Fore! Fore!"

The Choo-Choo Train of Breast Enhancement Technology, or Whiplash as Evidence of the Doppler Effect

bigger   better

        bigger   better

                bigger   better

                        bigger   better

                                bigger   better

                                      bigger better

                                          bigger better

                                              bigger better?

                                        bigger better

                                    bigger better

                              bigger   better

                        bigger   better

                bigger   better

        bigger   better

bigger   better

Oread–n. Gk. & Rom. Mythol. *a mountain nymph.*

Bored with those cranky mountain sages –
old, bearded hermits who don't appreciate
anything but new aches, a thousand sorrows

falling like the Heavens upon one's shoulders –
they snuck down under cover of cloud-banked
night, and wrecked havoc from the next

morning on, strutting into government offices
and junior high schools wearing clothes hoisted
from a local Sluts "Я" Us store: leather hot pants,

stiletto heels, chainlink belts, iridescent yellow
lipstick. Lonely after centuries of nothing to do
but catch bolts of lightning in their teeth as the titans

had done so long ago, the oreads wanted again
to feel the burn of male hands on them, as Prometheus
and his brother often did in the oilskin-dark days

of the Dragon, before the Big Sky War where the world
drank blood like the sweet nectar of ambrosia,
the gods' bodies littering the land, such divine carnage.

Purpose now renewed, the oreads sashayed wherever
they wanted, skanked up to the gills, snapping heads
with their end-of-the-world curves, legs which spoke

in a language of grace, eyes that shed details best
left to triple X movies. And like the Pied Piper of Hamelin,
these hussies led all the men up to the thin-aired snow

mountains, icy land of their birth; not one follower frowned, thinking how could such fleshy delights and blissful body-Braille evenings be the beginning of the beginning of the end?

An Elementary School Friend Writes to Britney

You, me, Happy Samantha,
and Preppy Lisa – remember
us in the midnight-blue sedan,
firing Silly String up each other's
skirts after your McBirthday party
at the mall? Later that December,
you taught me that words hurt
more than a first-degree burn,
like when you lifted the lid
on my mother's broccoli casserole
and the skin on your wrist rolled
into translucent veils I longed
to taste with the tip of my tongue.
It's true, you were right – I was
fat and too willing to seek sweetness
in a world which wasn't that sour.
So sue me. We were all dumb.
Thinking of you now is like
an armless man trying to spin
his wedding ring on a phantom finger.
I don't know if you still remember
that you stole my green shoelaces
or that you were a hog-ugly crier.
Sometimes I dream that you take
the barrel of your father's .38 in your mouth
after every packed stadium show –
but I'm no psychic. Still, I study you
in perfume commercials with your new
Grace Kelly smile and satyr eyes,
and there's always the paparazzi
nonsense about your husband parade.
　　　　Write back or not.

But whatever you do, you'll never entirely
airbrush out the scar on your ankle
from my soccer cleats. Same with
the lead pencil warhead in the palm
of your left hand. One day, I hope you'll
stand atop Caesar's in Vegas, arms wide,
ready to soar. And I'll be here, back home,
feeling feathers sprout from the silence of my body.
Will you think of me, then, as we collapse together?

Dante's Second Circle

Obsolete

I'm trying to convince my contemporary American literature
        students they're really missing something by not having seen
Amadeus, Raiders of the Lost Ark, and *Kramer vs. Kramer*,
            while they're arguing hard for *Deuce Bigalow, Male
Gigolo* and some movie called *Joe Dirt*, and it makes me think
about how things we once valued don't matter in the future;

just today, Tommie Smith put his 1968 Olympic gold medal up
        for auction, admitting it'd just been gathering dust
at the bottom of his sock drawer for thirty-three years.
           I was whining about this tragedy in our State Street
Starbucks when the couple a table over said, *Who's Tommie
Smith?* They were ten years older than me, but I had to explain

how Tommie Smith won the 200 meter and during the national anthem,
        gave the Black Power salute to honor the 30 Mexico City
University students killed a week before the Olympics
           when a campus protest turned into a race riot. I added,
*That was also the year Dick Fosbury won the high jump with his
Fosbury Flop, incidentally*, to which they said together, numbly, *Oh*.

My father had this problem, too – realizing what you value means
        just two winks shy of *nada* – when he told me Frank Sinatra
was the bluebird of enchantment; the voices that knifed upwards
           through me were Billy Squier, Sting, and early Michael
Jackson. Realizing now the distress my father must've felt then
is like a Wagner orchestral swelling in my gut that won't become

pianissimo. I'm twenty-nine, no longer hip enough to convince
        my students I know things like, *Waxing poetic in a moment
of romantic ecstasy, the rapper Shaggy said, "Closer than my peeps
           you are to me,"* because I thought "peeps" meant "eyes,"
but later realized it was cool-tough-rich-rapper slang for
"people," as in *Have your people call my people – we'll do lunch*.

Just last week, I tried to explain poetic juxtaposition via that Reese's
	Peanut Butter Cup commercial where some ape's in the jungle
	munching peanut butter, and Tarzan comes wailing in on a vine
		while devouring a chocolate bar, and they slam together,
	chocolate bar falls into peanut butter, and voilà, a tasty snack better
	than individual components, the sum much yummier than the parts.

They gave me a communal *Huh?* though I **know** they've seen repeats
	of those old candy commercials off and on . . . but maybe they
	didn't, I'm wondering. Freud wrote *Every dream is a wish*, and
		lately, I've been dreaming I was twenty again, the days
	like notes rising soft off Yo-Yo Ma's cello, so ethereal, but still
	chopping through the air like a mammoth meat cleaver. Is it me?

Am I that frumpled, whiny university professor one year short of thirty?
		This is your Actual Life, my father laughs at me over the phone.
	Welcome. And I think ultimately it's *Sesame Street*'s fault, them
		and MTV, jointly severing the attention span of children
	with quick-hitter lessons, jam-packed x-rated x-treme videos,
	constant action, eye-popping entertainment. Case in point,

Marie the ΣΣΣ in that literature class, who goes, takes notes, stares
	at me for ninety minutes, then emails me three days later
	asking what's due the next week. Neruda had it right, we're
		all unmasted ships crisscrossing the sea's fury – the men
	aboard grapple their memories, the final tatters of their ship,
	but still they know no matter what they do, no matter who cares,

the trajectory of everything, everyone, is always down.

PG-13

Maybe it's the mental image of seven dead grandmas
ghosting over me, their knitting needles clicking
in arthritic disapproval, or perhaps it's my Midwestern

sensibilities, a.k.a. a remarkable ability at self-deception,
but my sexual poems dribble out like piss struggling past
kidney stones, eyes clenched shut, forehead veins popping

under the strain. I want to write about Oreck blowjobs,
testicles that are a ready-to-burst steam engine left
unattended while some goober munches green Skittles,

eyes glued to channel 187. I want to write about lovers
who shuck their clothes and magnetize each other, a harp
of shadows strengthening to turbulence, then to plane-going-down

ferocity. Forget you-know-who's "sober lingering progress"
or that-other-nature-poet-fella's "topography of the soul," I want
wall-socket sex, legs V'd like a flight of geese heading thataway,

cries of "slamma-jamma-ding-dong!" from the bedroom.
And is it too much to want to write about a night of daiquiris
that ends in fishnet, garbage bags, and a red-haired girl known

to Cleveland as The Crotch Rocket? Here's the truth – I want
to lay in the arms of my wild cousin Nora the Exotic Dancer
and skinny dip my tongue in her quadruple-pierced ears,

stuff my hand inside the mattress of her tattooed thighs, teach her
how to conjugate me in nineteen different romance languages at once,
putting my Ph.D. to work at last as I scribble forbidden kisses

on her neck. Anything but a sonnet about passion fruit,
or two redwoods whose unseen roots intertwine in the dark,
moist earth while bees pollinate petunias lazily in the distance.

Benevolence: A Love Story Between Britney Spears and Animal from The Muppets

Britney read him Rod McKuen.

    He read her the ingredients from Cocoa Puffs.

She bought him a ghosted adobe ranch.

    He bought her Newman's Fat-Free Ranch dressing, but ate it himself.

She walked among garden-grown red salvia, violet daisies.

    He loped after the neighbor's line of cattle.

She gave him an earthquake of love.

    He thumped on his drums so hard, he didn't feel a thing.

She let him sniff her red latex catsuit.

    He ordered her a Superfly Animal 80s t-shirt off eBay.

She taught him dance moves from a Planet Phunk video.

    He teased her by twirling drumsticks with his tongue.

She showed him her first platinum album.

    He ground new grooves into them with his old record player.

She yanked angrily on his strings.

    He asked her to do it again.

She said she wanted an annulment.

    He grinned, urinating hot upon her leg.

Monica Lewinsky on the Banks of the River Styx:
A Schoolhouse Rock Homage

Staring into the inky waterface,
 she scrutinizes herself, the wild
  sweet of her eyes, the soft
   talc desert of her cheeks.

She'd hoped to find Lethe,
 the river of forgetting,
  whose bitter waters wipe
   clean the slate of memory,

might, at last, erase the Jubjub
 bird, that dark demon
  which hounds her night
   and day, its terrible cry

that echoes in her mind:
 I'm just a Bill,
  Yes, I'm only a Bill,
   And I'm sitting here at Capitol Hill.

Roger Is Famous

he'd say about himself
in the third person,
this tousle-haired eight-
year-old with a lunch pail
grin and hand-me-down
jeans. We were in home
room together. I offered
him my 3-D sticker collection
to be in the next Juicy Juice
commercial with him, even
if I was just the anonymous
hand in the corner of the screen
that filled the glass Roger
was about to drink before
igniting his 3,000 watt smile.

Roger is a liar, I realized
before long. A blue convertible
Camaro was not in the garage
waiting until he turned 16.
He didn't have Heather
Locklear's sister for a mom.
He didn't travel each summer
to Maui, London, or Hong Kong.
He did have a special bus, though,
a thirty-foot silver Airstream
that went into Bradford Forest
to pick him up by the lake
and shuttle him alone to school.

We all rarely spoke to him,
but when we bothered to, called
him by his full name, "Roger Is Famous."

"Hey, Roger Is Famous, what's
for lunch today?" or "Roger Is
Famous got a C in gym class!"
Two years later, Roger's voice
imploded into a hormonal
screech. He grew gangly,
and his face became an acne
minefield, a constant crimson
eruption thanks to his nervous
fingers. No more special bus.
No more Roger Is Famous
at all. Moved to a different
school district perhaps, a place
higher in altitude so he might
suckle the empty air of his life
for stray starlight, chance
patches of light that might,
if viewed cockeyed, appear
to be centered on him.

Famous (Almost)

Up until the hearse hauls him away,
      my brother will seek fame, a moment
      of drinking Red Bull from the glitzy cups
      of Madonna's pointy bra, ninety minutes of bloodying
himself before a suckling, gurgling, mooing
      crowd, a single day whose cross-section is pork-
      white, pulpy and sweet without question.
      Sure, he's right – *Music is the epidermis of the soul.*
A pulsing bass drum and chunka-chunka raunch
      of a balls-out Les Paul socks you in the teeth,
      the subcutaneous fat, the pit cavities of your bones.
      But what slaps the Ray-Bans off his face
is the definition of roar, the rise and spiral down
      of a mob's one voice, how it lowers the rope
      of his life into a rich, dark well once more.
      I visited him last week, the smell of bourbon
rank in the carpet, cigarette butts spearing
      the soil of a dead potted fern. Beneath the bed,
      the ashes of his old bandmate, the Speedball King,
      cooled in a Nike box. My brother put on
Iggy Pop vinyls, and we listened, the clogged
      snarl through pop-crackle speakers pushing us apart,
      bringing us back, like debris caught in a wave.

Urban Stalkers, or Celebrity Photographers at Night

Flashbulbs popping like the explosion of distant galaxies, Sly Stallone and two leggy brunettes in sequins hurry from the Hollywood Hard Rock Café and duck into an almond-colored limousine that roars away. Twenty minutes later, coming from a four-star teriyaki house on Sepulveda, Rick Moranis walks into the firing line of telephoto lenses, boom microphones, and coked-up men from the supermarket tabloids waving exclusive story contracts like they were fanning Marilyn on the hottest day of the decade. As a child, I wanted to be a celebrity photographer for *The National Enquirer* because I wanted my name attached to stories like "Three-Headed Gypsy Woman Cures Cancer . . . with Campbell's Chicken Soup" and "Lose 30 lbs. in Thirty Minutes Flat – New Miracle Pill Derived from Alien DNA." Plus there was something about "paparazzi," how the word fizzes in the lips like a smooth Jack and Coke. The late media analyst Marshall McLuhan claimed all media must be understood as an extension of the human nervous system, and this makes sense to me when I sleep, my hands curled into shells, and I dream of the blood pulsing in my veins as, 35mm Pentax in hand, I whisper to Madonna her secret name: *Romanoff.* Behind fake glasses and removable beard, it's easy to imagine anyone skulking with me in the azalea bushes, treasuring the hours of loneliness as Governor Schwarzenegger stuffs his face with pineapple pizza at some upstairs Italian joint in Sacramento. Indeed, as I linger this evening in the chiaroscuro shadows of a convent wall, waiting for Steven Spielberg to meet with his private orthopedic surgeon, the nerves in my hands are assaulted by stimuli, the prick of rose-thorns, the damp night air, the rills and gorges of moonlight that settles upon me. For a moment, I'm a creature of water, a turtle clambering ashore on a beach in the middle of nowhere – it's not so much that I don't know what I am, but rather that with a lock of Kim Basinger's hair twisted around my finger, I'm no longer gawky and gap-toothed, and I can trick the flower of my life into blooming once again.

Simon Says

You sang like someone who sings on a cruise ship.
    Halfway through, I imagined the ship sinking.

I think you invented notes never ever heard before in music.

Phone up your vocal coach and demand a refund.

You sang like a ventriloquist dummy.

You don't need a judge – you need an exorcist.

Ryan [Seacrest], an ooompa-loompa called and wants its complexion back.

You're so terrible, you're not even good enough for *Bulgarian Idol*.

Don't take this the wrong way, but I prefer you when I close my eyes.

If your lifeguard duties were as good as your singing, a lot of people would be drowning.

If you would have sung like this two thousand years ago, people would have stoned you.

When you stopped singing – *that* was the best part.

Kong Speaks: A Three-Part Nocturne

Part 1 – *Such Hunger*

There's not corn, evergreen bark,
and mutton for soup enough
to curb the undiminished dark
that drums so deep in my chest.
Once, I surrendered to its rhythm,
tore apart a young boy from
the village who cried, *Rama Kong,*
Rama Kong! His meat was tough,
a clash of gristle and sinew that
made me splinter an old alligator
bone for a toothpick. I am lonely,
hungry, and wondering if the moon
would steep some river water
and buzzard beaks into a nice,
luscious black tea like Momma
Kong used to make.

Part 2 – *The Lost Spider Scene*

Bleaching the landscape,
a horde of albino spiders
crawled out one night
from the northern caves,
a grave sheet of white
I murdered with a stack
of boulders, a tree I ripped
from the ground and swung
until my arms began to ache.
Truth be told, I am afraid
of arachnids, how they skitter
and climb, so many glittering
eyes watching you at once.
I would rather try to swallow
the ocean than let them swarm me,
their eyes greening with desire.

Part 3 – *Thorns, Shadows*

I have always wanted to sing,
to let my voice reverberate across
the treetops and clouds, but I am
not lovely, and I am aware that
the tones from my throat are harsh,
screeching, unpleasant. Some nights
I sit beneath the avalanche of stars
and swallow wild berries by the fistful,
letting the juice purple my lips, my neck.
Fool that I am, I dare hope this sweetness
will become the ceremony of my life,
that my shadow will no longer be
ominous, my eyes not darken
with the crush of bone. I just want
my voice to be anything but a thunderdrum.
Grief after grief, the days pass, but still
I pray to the god of change, fool
that I am, fool that I cannot help but be.

The Birds and the Bees

Hastily agreed to after a fifty-dollar

bribe from the single neighbor

woman, I sit Richard Jr. on the cement

stoop of my back porch, and try

as I might not to, all I think of is George

Washington in polyester pants

leaning against a green VW bug, wooden

teeth clacking away as he speaks

of God's plan for the people of America

and how paragraph 6, subsection

11, lines 3-6 of the Philadelphia Procreation

Act of 1782 is the answer.

I swallow thickly, toy with the pink and

gold hibiscus my wife planted

after seeing them on that stucco terrace

in *Aladdin*. "It's like those oil

derricks in Texas. Have you ever seen

them in the movies, those big

metal dealies?" He says no. I bring up

refrigerated trucks, sausages,

shoelaces, but no dice, *nada*, zip.

I collapse in the grass, feeling

a lot like Ben, my high school pal who

now is a lousy conversationalist

thanks to drugs, when Richard Jr. says,

"Have you ever rimmed a girl?"

to which I say, "What?" and this eight-

year-old explains how it's when

you take your tongue and tease circles

around some poor girl's asshole,

literally. It was a moment fiercely

reminiscent of the time in an

Olive Garden that I noticed Aunt Mary's

                                                      nipples poking from her blouse

like two nuclear warheads ready

                                                      to put me out of my misery. I ruffle

Richard Jr.'s hair, then send him home

                                                      while I hasten inside to

the shower, unable to cast off my clothes

                                                      fast enough, thinking all

the while that neighbors are neighbors for

                                                      a reason and any impromptu

intersection of familiarity is just an icy

                                                      street with a malfunctioning

stoplight that's just hungering for a bloody

                                                      crash, a tangle of bodies that

shares one breath, then slows, falters, then

                                                      stops altogether, just like that.

The Seven Deadly Sins

The Pride Poem

I'd like to think a 105 IQ could fire neurons fast enough,
    even as you break knuckles pounding down death's door,
to come up with last words better than James Thurber, "God bless . . .
God damn . . ." or H. G. Wells, who groaned, "Go away . . . I'm all right."
    And one evening, as the Green Bay skyline bleeds for a moment
  into medusa-tongue purple, I grow reflective and wonder if I should

change my name as one girlfriend suggested after trying to spell
    it four times on the phone to a Domino's delivery guy.
After all, she said, Stevie Wonder did it (from Steveland Judkins
Morris), as did Michael Caine (Maurice Mickelwhite) and even John
    Denver (Henry John Deutschendorf, Jr.). A trio of gulls
  explode from the poplars quick as brush strokes upon an empty sky,

and I fancy my moniker reminiscent of Van Morrison, Van Cleef
    & Arpel, Van Halen. "There are options, and there are
options," I tell myself aloud, thinking of all the infinite zeros
the lives of my high school buddies have become despite so many
    plans to shake the dust from the earth's face with glory
  and innovation. True, I haven't cured cancer, yet, and the Pulitzer

committee hasn't sent me that giant cardboard check and secret vial
    of immortality ink, but as my father once said, "The world
is a Black Angus cow and you're no vegetarian," and he's right,
dammit. Copernicus might've been the first person to butter his bread,
    but Winston Churchill nailed it: "We are all worms, but I do
  believe I'm a glow worm." It's not the idle philosophy

of nomenclature or a firm belief that I'm attached to the universe
          by an unseen navel string called destiny, but rather a sense
of relevance that I feel about my life, the same sense of mattering
that Tu Fu felt when Li Po first wrote back: "Can any river possibly
          flow between the love of friends?" Sure, my father doesn't believe
     in pride, claims it's the black-eyed crow perched in a yew tree,

watching you watching it watching you. "Steer clear of anything
          that makes you feel bigger than you are," my father added
once while lugging a lightning-downed sapling to the front yard
where a woodchipper chunked into life. And perhaps that's why
          I'm reluctant to tell my wife my latest poetry book has been
     accepted for publication, or that I won three hundred bucks in Lotto.

It's hard not to wonder if secret smugness such as this is just me
          foolishly devouring fruit that's fallen from the tree, food that no bird
wants. Like Aquinas, I think of mind, body, the whispery cries that
might perhaps maybe be my soul, yearning to rear up, show
          at last its finely sculpted head. Look – there are facts and there are
     facts. A brick and a plate-glass window are both made from sand.

There are two hundred billion molecules in a cubic centimeter
          of air. In a pinch, Coca-Cola can be used in a car instead of oil.
Surely it means something that I know these things, that I might be
the only person in Green Bay who does. Surely it means something that
          the last words of Dylan Thomas were, "I've had 18 straight
     whiskeys. I think that's a record!" Surely Nietzsche was an optimist,

promising: *What does not destroy me, makes me strong.*

SIN POEM #2

The Envy Poem

Having been identified early on as a Potential Behavior Problem
(by my parents, preschool teacher, postman, anorexic neighbor lady,
   etc.), I was inundated with advice, mostly from my father, whose
words of wisdom were like slow-trigger booby traps. Put too much
      weight, too much faith in them, and BOOM, down you'd go.

But what stuck with me was this nugget: whenever you feel yourself
start to envy someone else, count from twenty down to one, letting
   the numbers come with each breath, every pulse through your body –
let the resentment just leak away. And so I did. When the burnout girl
      from high school won a half-mil in the lottery, *twenty, nineteen,*

eighteen, it was as if I were peeling a thin skin of spite right off
of me, exfoliating the anger, which made me think of zen, how
   sparrows scatter-shoot from a willow oak in infinite trajectories
that only a Buddhist understands, finding fragments of himself in
      the blueprint of action. I longed for that peace, that deep

silence, especially after an ex-sweetheart transformed from a sputtering
gas-jet of banter to a Dr. Atkins-slimmed wonder, an exotic jungle
   bird who finally allowed her wings to fold at last *seventeen, sixteen, fifteen*
into the arms of someone else. At sixteen, having inherited a small
      fortune and wanting to increase it exponentially, I put it all behind

the makers of The Tamahonam, a Hong Kong virtual pet with Mob
connections. Instead of feeding him by pressing buttons, you ply
   him with booze and cigarettes. And in lieu of playing with him,
you give him a little plastic knife to "wage turf battles," which to me
      sounded like the toy that would have made me, anyone, king

of the block. My friends from work *fourteen, thirteen, twelve* invested
in Coleco, who made Cabbage Patch dolls . . . And somewhere
    in my fair to middlin' high school years, I learned that in 1221, Genghis
Khan is said to have killed over a million people in one hour. "That's
        impressive," I told a pair of friends. One said I should be

committed. The other *eleven, ten, nine* admitted years later that he
was joking, but at the time had said my most important contribution
    to the world would be a bowel movement so powerful that I'd die
of a brain aneurysm. About that same time, eighteenish, I developed
        an affinity for sunsets, would travel for hours to distant

spots to watch the sky momentarily turn into a fiery lake, such
reds and oranges, these corncobs of bright. And I tried to remember
    that peace I felt *eight, seven, six,* as all my friends received college
scholarships but not me, and that my rock band didn't hit it big
five, four, three, while my brother's band, Rubber, rakes in a quarter
        mil a year, under-the-table cash, tax-free. Clearly God is

trying my patience, lingering behind a bamboo curtain *two, one, zero,*
until I learn this lesson: all bones are deadwood, every roof a coffin
    lid. How we handle the rest is how we sift through the ashes
of the earth. Until today, I've brushed the grit from my sleeves
and howled in outrage. Now I want to go at it with a broom, like
        my father did, like his father did, and try to see just what

the hell's beneath this cinder landscape, and find out whether
that voice I sometimes hear is God fanning his fingers, thinking
    of me, counting slowly down from twenty to nothing at all.

The Anger Poem, or Hatred as Brass-Boned Monster

The first person I ever hated was Patrick Ewing, the former center
        for the New York Knicks. During an impending N.B.A.
work stoppage, a reporter asked him, "Eight sports cars. Fourteen
sports cars. Three million a year. Nine million a year. When's
        it all enough?" Ewing smoothed a wrinkle in his peach Italian

silk shirt and replied, "Sure, we make a lot of money. But we **spend**
        a lot of money." Okay, okay, he wasn't the first person I loathed,
but rather the first famous person I've wanted to sucker punch, then beat
the hell out of with an aluminum bat and feed him his own onions.
        It'd kill my kind-hearted parents to know this, but I confess there's

something exhilarating about getting angry, I mean Biblical fuming, real
        Old Testament stuff where the lug nuts to your own infernal engine
fly off and the curse words blast out as if from a firehose, and the world
becomes a faint red shadow in which your body is the only thing that's
        rippling. Just imagine the lightning bolts scorching the air around

Thomas Hardy's sister. His heart was to be buried in Stinsford, England,
        his birthplace, after the rest of his body was cremated in Dorchester.
And as she was packing his heart in butcher paper, her cat snatched it
off the kitchen table and disappeared into the woods for good.
        Just think of the president of General Mills in the late 1960s

who learned that topping their new breakfast product line was Day-
        O, the world's first calypso-inspired presweetened cereal. More
than all that, I hate James Pace, the idiot handyman from Tallahassee
who took my money but didn't fix that broken window, then called
        the cops because my "harassment phone calls" were scaring

his pregnant wife. And I hate Darryl Strawberry and Rod McKuen,
        for obvious reasons, but most of all I hate Osama bin Laden,
not because he took out the WTC with a boatload of folks who were
minding their Ps and Qs, but because my mother is too scared to
        shop at the grocery store anymore. Try to convince her

that any future terrorist attack won't be at the Jewel/Osco
        in a suburb some twenty miles to the northwest of Chicago,
and she weighs the options Libra-like, holding two empty hands
before her and testing the heft of air until one hand drops, the other
        raises, and she says, "No, thank you," and stays home, hungry,

huddled in an afghan her mother didn't quite finish before she
        died alone, three weeks after moving into a senior care home.
Surely God would let the stars dazzle like jewels of satisfaction
if I put on green war paint, took a Rambo M-60 in hand, and blasted
        Osama's arms off. Surely my third-grade teacher who said

I'd "never amount to anything but a world of potential" would then
        take her three cats by the paws and dance all night to Stevie
Wonder songs. Surely my folks would be proud if I took that
terror-maker by the throat and gave him the chokecherry, a wrestling
        move my high school buddy invented that actually worked

and had KO'd a half-dozen sixteen-year-olds before it was banned
        from Palatine High School. Surely all the fury I'd built up
over thirty years would be poured into that broken, cracked vessel
of a man, leaving me whole again, the secret code of hatred unlearnt,
        my ghost-blossom of anger sent fleeing to distant, tropical skies.

SIN POEM #4
The Sloth Poem

For six weeks, I've been writing a poetic series on the Seven Deadly
      Sins, and I've left this poem for the end, having felt inspiration
cool like a campfire left to sputter out overnight. The muse of my sins
      has begun a crawl back to the past on knees, hands, a child again
      who refuses to think, or cry, or play fair at all. Look, I'm

the laziest mother out there, perfectly content to play Xbox all day and
      ignore Arthur Schopenhauer – it's my right, after all, to scratch
the days off my calendar a few weeks ahead. And I can stay silent,
      trusting Nietzsche who wrote, "The author must keep his mouth
      shut when his work starts to speak." But fearing such quiet, I

plow on, finding refuge in my wife's advice: "Everyone loves a
      palindrome." So in lieu of chasing down the muse, and dragging
her back caveman-like by her thick, oily hair, here are my wife's three favs:
      (1) Campus motto: Bottoms up, Mac. (2) Oh, no – Don Ho!
      (3) Satan, oscillate my metallic sonatas. Impressive, perhaps,

but not as much as the all-time champion anagram. "To be or not to be,
      that is the question. Whether 'tis nobler in the mind to suffer
the slings and arrows of outrageous fortune" handily becomes
      "In one of the bard's best-thought-of tragedies, our insistent
      hero, Hamlet, queries on two fronts about how life turns

rotten." I wrote this on a high school English exam once because I hadn't
      read *Othello* and couldn't answer the essay question. My teacher
wrote: "I am suitably impressed, but you have not, however,
      demonstrated in any way that you actually **read** *Othello*
      and understand it, let alone prepare yourself well for essay exams."

True, true, but there's more to life than high school exams, something Fiona
            Apple knows, saying, "I'm a mess and you're a mess, too. Everyone's
a mess. Which means, actually, that no one's a mess," which really doesn't
            have anything to do with Shakespeare or test-taking for that matter,
            but a *non sequitur* is its own *raison d'être*, no? Seriously,

though, I have been thinking lately of motionlessness, of how a body
            might slow to a stop such that every molecule, every germ,
every flesh-atom stills and defies physics in a moment of anti-clocktickery
            and each bit of me will remember the lives it participated in
            before, everything prior to the dark sand island where I didn't

ask to be born. Is it autobiography to hum floral notes and think
            of embedding ourselves in the text of the past? Is this the same
as snuffing out candle after candle to find darkness worthy enough
            for sleep? Is this the type of journey that becomes a song
            that lingers, nagging like small bits of debris in the eye?

"Live not on evil, madam, live not on evil," the palindromist might
            say before downing an Italian sub with extra onions and
a pepperoni periscope that lets him glimpse God during an all-nighter
            on the bathroom floor. Lying there, perhaps, he'll know what it is
            to be breath without body, cheeseburger without cheese. Maybe,

too, he'll hear my wife's voice (as I always do), infiltrating his gastrointestinal
            haze: *Oozy rat in a sanitary zoo.*

SIN POEM #5

The Avarice Poem, or After Reading Martín Espada's Imagine the Angels of Bread, *I Want to Kick His Ass*

And it's for the worst reason ever: greed.
                    By God, I'm the greediest mother you
could ever meet. I want to sneak into his *casa*,
                    drub him silly right there on the couch,
even if he surrenders, pleading, *Take the poems! They're yours!*
                    For years, I've been hoarding ideas like an
insatiable spinster, ways to have written my own "Author's Note:
                    Hands Without Irons Become Dragonflies" or
"Imagine the Angels of Bread" (the poem). It's
                    just that *Señor Espada* beat me to it,
knifing my ideas in the back one by one by one,
                    like a bowling ball mowing down so many pins.
More and more, I realize I'm not at all well,
                    not that anybody whose heart resembles an
open cave *is* well, but I want to soar *como un buitre*,
                    play "Moonlight" like Thelonious Monk,
quaff gin in dark alleys with Bukowski and Hemingway.
                    Right now, I polish my hand-me-down
silver wing-tips and wonder if I've gone *loco*, bonkers,
                    totally fried in the neurons, but I'm simply
unable to say, *Bravo, Martín. ¡Buena Suerte!* (You lucky fella)
                    ¡Viva la poesía! ¡Viva Martín! I want to have
won the American Book Award. I want to bang the
                    xylophone of society like an athiest at God's door.
You can't talk sense to a brick wall, my father always said, *so just*
                    zip up your trap. Reason-proof: my pure, lowly greed.

SIN POEM #6
The Gluttony Poem

On some kind of self-destructive binge after learning my cholesterol
hit 220 again, I have been listening to *Sebastian Speaks! Your
Watchdog on a Disc* (by Grr-r Records) for three days, which contains
thirty minutes of menacing canine noises. The record jacket
claims "No stand-in dogs or sound effects were used." My wife is very

concerned, as much that a record like this exists as the fact that I own it and
am listening to it, but I am thirty and overweight, having given in to
my love for mango pie and blackberry & smoked turkey sandwiches
and chocolate chunk ice cream ten too many times. At twenty-two,
I went on a Coca-cola bender for a week after finding out I had asthma

the same day I saw *The Conqueror*, starring John Wayne as an extremely
sauced Genghis Khan who sports a Fu Manchu moustache and tapes his
eyes to give him a "somewhat Asian" look. The part was designed for
Brando's stylized archaic Elizabethan English like he used in *Julius
Caesar*, but he was booked so the Duke got the part and had to say lines

like "I am bereft of spirit" and "I feel this Tartar woman is for me. My
blood says take her." When asked how he planned to play a 12th century
Mongol warlord, Wayne answered, "I see him as a gunfighter." Enough
said. And for eight years, I've wheezed away evenings remembering
one moment, years earlier, where I stood freshly shaven in the moonlight

with a 7-11 bean burrito in one hand, a moment I imagine the Duke could
appreciate, a real me-and-this-weapon-of-destruction-against-the-world
mentality. Funny or not, food has been my weapon of choice, a lifelong
ode to a gluttonous future. The streets run red with the juice of
tomatoes, cherries, raspberries, such inexhaustible bright these stars

of the earth. Give me bread enough, and a knife, and I'll sweep the
yard clean, wash the ocean stones of oysters and clams, shake the pigeons
   and pheasants from the air while stormclouds brew in the distance,
         threatening a Genesis-style world-washing, and I feel myself begin
to burst at the seams, my soul billowing heavy in the darkening wind.

Yes, Neruda was right, *un solo cuerpo, uno enemigo*, one body, one enemy.
And it's a slow, slow journey that we're now beginning, together,
   mouth wide as a fresh-split melon dusted lightly with salt.

The Lust Poem

Britney again, sometimes Madonna (the Material Girl not the Material
Mom), and often Shania Twain (those silver shorts – yikes!) and Julia
    Roberts, with silken legs that run from here to next Thursday. These
        are the birds who sing through the jungle haze of my life,
the war they don't realize they're waging. Crepuscular angels, soft

metals that join together into one shimmering ring I reach for, Phoebe-
like, again and again, stretching so far from the ridiculous carousel
    horse upon which I am perched. It can be difficult to sleep at night,
        thinking of the dangerous hairpin curve of such buttocks,
the gooseflesh prickling around hard nipples caused by the dream-me

(nicer, better looking, taller, and much closer to Einstein in IQ than
the fella from *Sling Blade* who just wanted taters and biscuits). My wife
    does not understand these unannounced longings, the mystic rubies
        I keep hidden in my wallet to gaze at like pages of some ancient
philosophy, strips of old pear bark that carry the spirit of a long-dead saint.

Look, the main speaker at Gettysburg ran two hours, Lincoln clocked two
minutes. I'd like my life to go like Lincoln's hundred and twenty seconds,
    a wheatfield silvered in cloudburst, a landscape right out of a medieval
        love song that whispers passion to the rain. And so I tell my wife,
I'll strut-drum on a branch with the best of the red-caps, but in my heart

of hearts, if Shania called me up and said she wanted to play naked
Twister, I'd have to strongly consider it. Still, I don't worry that
    this particular truth hurts my wife, because I know the windstorm
        that thrums the window of her heart whispers words we all
know: *Brad Pitt, Antonio Banderas, Ricky Martin.* And sure as Pope

Leo X had a pet elephant (he did), I'm certain most folks in America
have a mental list of seven to a dozen people who coax their waking
   hours, could threaten marriages if only these distant, beautiful
            paragons but knew. The years have made us all what we are,
and before long I'll have to limp my way around the bases,

perhaps throw a duck-handled cane down before sliding
into home plate, but even as the arthritic bones in my legs
   snap like kindling and my hip-joints give out, I'll finally know
            the applause of pop idols as my secret harem
claps, Madonna and Julia sharing a Diet Coke alfresco, Shania

tumbling onto the grassy field in some extra-teensy cheerleader
skirt, and Britney, the precious precocious one, will swagger
   in the stands, shake that billion-dollar booty, and smile,
            letting new auburn hair flare about her, a firestorm
against the cool white of an unseen sky worth waiting forever for.

Aphrodite in America

Drive-In: A Narrative

The mayor's son, Willis, and his sidekick, Mouse,
still head up most weekends to the Princess Drive-In
where they used to sell Milk Duds and buckets of pop,

only now they take Mouse's open-air Lincoln –
though rusty, it's midnight blue, the same color as the one
JFK was shot in. In the shadowhive of its trunk, they've hidden

cartons of month-old eggs and a potato sack that squirms.
During a hot sex scene, they tear that sack open
and release a confused raccoon into the maze of pickups

just to hear girls howl and watch Benny, the ancient security
guard, wave his flashlight as he probes beneath cars
for "that beast." Willis played two seasons on the Chicago Bears

practice squad and still has a quarterback's arm, the ability to lose
himself in the motion of a tight spiral. Mouse titters,
crouching low in the seat, while Willis zings egg after egg

at Tom Cruise's eyes, *crack crack crack* like the snare drum
during September marching band practice. Some yahoo
from upstate finally sicced his bloodhound on them, yelling,

"Teach 'em a thing or three, Harris!" Willis snatched up
a length of garden hose from behind the snack bar and beat
that dog like torturing a confession from a terrorist bomber.

Benny has his hand deep into the Slushee machine, letting
Razzberry Blue cool the pair of raccoon bites. No one
calls the police because Willis is the mayor's son; everyone

knows there's something hard in him, an ominous ticking
like that clock in the belly of the crocodile chasing Captain Hook.
It's no secret that the icy ocean he's drowning in is the shore

of their town, the cold forcing their mouths into Os as though
yawning, all the air run arctic at last.

The Flash, in Old Age

Mostly he just watches the circling ocean birds
as he sits in a porch rocker near the Pacific,
looking for blue everlasting. His childhood
friends no longer swing by to visit, being
otherwise committed. Green Lantern chases
his devil-may-care kids, Jade and Obsidian,
to all ends of the earth. Wonder Woman, Dr. Fate,
Hawkman, and the rest still run the Justice
Society of America, which isn't easy thanks
to Johnny Thunder and The Black Canary
drinking the Elixir of Evil along with Grodd
and Captain Cold. Worse, the speed clones
who emerged like safety pins into the heart
of The Flash are still at work, chasing down
bullets from behind, zipping from his failing sight
like darkness lost between rocks. The Whizzer.
Quicksilver. And McSnurtle the Turtle (a.k.a.
The Terrific Whatzit). Jay Garrick – The Flash –
considered reimmersing himself in the deadly
chemical fumes that superhero-ized him as a
college sophomore, but the voice of heaven
has been calling him, promising a place without
hunger or thirst. He is confused with feeling,
forced by gravity and aching muscles at last
to ponder stillness, the particular mundane
moments that make up the wholeness of a day.
As the sun sets again, he makes quarters vanish
from his hand; semi-speedy fingers are all that's
left of the blur that was his youth. Overhead,
the stars come to life, burning at the dark as strongly
as ever. But The Flash's heart does not beat faster.

Mike Tyson as the Old Man in Grant Wood's "American Gothic"

Having just gut-slugged
the plow horse for being
down with colic again, Mike
refused at first to pose
for a portrait before the
homestead his prizefighter
father built after being
brained with a coal shovel
outside Atlanta. Instead, Mike
slogged down to the stream
where he played as a boy,
empty now after three months
of drought, crumbling
with weeds and the husks
of water bushes. *It's one thing*
to let the wind roughen you,
said his father after giving
a beating, *but another thing*
entirely to stomp around
with the cutting knife
of bad luck clenched between
your teeth like you're some kind
of African war god. This was
before they argued over who
had to burn clear the pumpkin
fields and Mike ended it with
a pitchfork thrust that tore
through his father's gullet
too easily, draining his heart.
After brooding for hours whether
it was worth two buckets of milk
to let Grant Wood, a painter

neighbor, capture his likeness,
Mike gave in and let himself
be depicted against the mounting
dusk, demanding only two
things: *Let my father's shadow*
hide among the treetops in the
horizon, and please oh please,
whatever you do, don't paint
me here alone as I am among
the parched earth and the aimless
sigh of an always-easterly wind.

For Britney's Makeup Artist

After three years on the road, she still
dreams of tree-high tiaras and a freeway
shadow that doesn't darken her back porch.
At each new supermarket, she buys apricots
to dry and grind into powder.
At the main street flea markets,
great peacock feathers for application.
Always, the night-watered geraniums
and wild mustard in the window box
to make sleeping poultices, orange oils
that create skin glow beneath a spotlight.
It's Christmas again, and she's dreaming
herself over – this time, she's in a red
flannel bathrobe and her father's frying
ham hocks in the kitchen while a handsome
son-in-law, her husband, sifts her hair
with his fingers and says, *Your eyes
are like baby stars.* Tonight, though,
her fingers interpret tomorrow's perfumes,
powders, and creams, testing it on the stuffed
flop-eared bunny, her own wrist, the trailer's
frosted back window. She finger-traces
a smiley in green mascara and wonders
how it'd feel to wear a diamond-studded
garter to bed just once, a half-million dollars'
worth glistening cold against her own skin.

Michael Jackson in the Underworld

No one told him
what such cataclysmic
heat could do to an
oxygen sleeping tube,
so understandably
he's a bit shaken,
and Lord knows he
understands the equation
oiled hair + open flame.
It's a dangerous venue
for Michael to moonwalk
there among the wasp-
faced demons and
hordes of legitimate
"Thriller" personnel,
but he's half in love
with Walt Whitman,
that cinder-coal specter
who whistles off-key
to "Billie Jean," and who
wouldn't want to do
the twist with Little
Richard and Patsy Cline's
pigeon-gray shade? Still,
the show has to end when
the fat banshee screams,
and Michael always
returns to his Never-
Never playland, slow-
crawling up the lava
chutes from the earth's
smoky gut, emerging
tired and marathon-drained

in his backyard treehouse
where no children laugh
and skull-faced guards
haunt his every move.
Sleepless and worn,
he's a tattered ghost
who gapes into a
splintered piece of mirror
and almost recognizes
a face that looks a bit
like someone who was
famous once, perhaps,
for a while.

The End of Karate Movies

Like a cake of lilac-smelling soap left too long
in steamy bathwater, this fad of chopping boards

in half and executing moves like the Dragon Wing Defense
or Grinning Leopard Flying Dropkick

is at its end, the pugilists and actors, those special-effect saints,
disappearing into the sea like all things archaic.

The door to the future is opened with a key, not
with nunchucks or an ear-splitting *Kiiiiiyyyyyaaaaaahhhhh ! ! !*

Jackie Chan will go back to stuffing grocery sacks
and my brother, the chung moo quan master, will instead

turn in his clam-colored robes and wild chestnut hair
for an M.B.A. from Roosevelt and a high-powered C.P.U.

Peace will descend like a slow fog over the land,
and everyone will be the better for it, drinking chai tea

and eating carb-friendly biscuits, everyone polite as a shogun's
wife. But when no one is watching, you might find me

out near the ocean, perhaps balancing one-legged on a pier
as I snapkick stars out of the sky to the sound of waves breaking.

Prenup

not because you pick names like Kaleb and Kori because you thought they
were types of rhododendrons, your grandmother's favorite

not because with feet like those you can dance on dynamite

not because the cameras are always filming – unrepentant like distant
polar stars

not because Walt Whitman never said, "Tip 'em a dime, the next time they
expect a quarter"

not because tender hooks can gouge out your eyes sure as mother's milk can
drown you

not because there are machines with a thousand gears which grind and
chug away, sucking the air out of an entire room, a house, an amphitheatre, an entire
line of longitude

not because Mickey Mouse says to love each other as you want to be
loved, and Lord knows Walt Disney loved Mickey more than any woman
he ever knew

not because lollipops in Vegas glow casino green and might be planted
in desert sand to someday, perhaps, with enough nuclear fallout, bloom
money-trees in perfect rows, a beautiful stretch of hundreds and
unmarked, non-consecutively serial-numbered twenties

not because mathematically speaking, parallel lines never quite connect
in this or any other universe

but simply because the backwaters of a heart crash hard against the jetty –
stones, even two-carat honkers, can only last so long against such
hurly-burly and tempestuousness

Dear Britney:
An Epithalamium for Marriage #2

As a child on a train to Antwerp,
you saw seahorses in the clouds
of an orangish sky – even the man
selling herring and fries couldn't
say no. Think, too, of talcum powder
that smells of lily mist, the blue lace
handkerchief you mother pressed
to your forehead during a fever spell,
the driveway gravel cold and sharp
beneath young, sockless feet.
In 1948, four men tried to take a cow
to the top of Mt. Everest, but they all
froze to death – don't let this news
dissuade you. Think instead of
fields of Flemish wheat, how blond tides
burn into the horizon, a blizzard
of yellow against coppery shadows
and skin-colored hills. Dear Mrs. Federline,
you know the answer to your own heart –
whether you're Cézanne speaking of Pissaro
or Bobby Fischer hiding away in Iceland,
1 + 1 in your weightless world always = 1.

The Saint of Emaciation

One of the neighbor girls has brought
home a St. Bernard puppy. After four
months, it's clear that Angie – a six-one
blonde who weighs 98 lbs., an eerily
beautiful figure with too few contours,
not enough horizontalness – has projected
her weight issues onto the dog she's calling
"Samson." "Like the Biblical figure?"
I asked. "No," she said. "Like my DVD
player." "That's Sam*sung*, as in S-U-N-G,"
I told her, to which she shrugged in her
pink floral dress, size zero, saying, "Well,
he doesn't know the difference." *Perhaps*
not, I tell myself, but he does know the difference
between empty and full, desire and satiation.
His ribs jut out like prison bars. His spindle-legs
explode downward into gigantic, awkward paws.
I palm him potato chips and thick slices off
a gouda wheel, but Samson remains weak,
tugging half-heartedly on the chain linking him
to the outside water spigot. This mid-December
morning arrives with three full inches
of fresh snow, a shellacking of ice over
the branches, incandescent spears hanging
low on all the gutters. Inside for now,
Samson presses his wet snoot up against window
glass, imagining a world of ice cream topped
with maraschino cherries and Snausage sprinkles;
his eyes close as a wide smile eases over
his dark, thin lips, and he stays that way, unmoving,
not a single gleeful bark from him now, ever.

Bubbles Speaks

Cultural Noise
or Captain Kirk and the Trouble with Kibble

I don't know which is worse, that my four dogs refuse to eat
   anything but premium-grade Kibbles 'n Chunks with Cheese,
or listening to my critic-friend lament the blitzkrieg of emails
from hungry young authors explaining for the hundredth time
        why their treatise on holistic vegetarianism is the "Left/

Progressive answer to Capitalist, meat-eating excesses of Our Time!!!"
   The whole book business has gone to hell, my friend continues, citing
a recent first novel blurb by Bret Easton Ellis which read, "Imagine
Britney Spears narrating *The Day of the Locust* as a gentle fable
        and you'll get the idea." One-way ticket to the big time, indeed.

And it's not that I don't sympathize with writers who have to scream like
   a howler monkey to rise above the constant din of cultural noise, but I
don't blame the self-publishing and print-on-demand book world, I blame
church bulletins. It's hard to take religion seriously, much less anything
        else, when the church I got married in runs announcements like:

"A bean supper will be held Saturday evening in the church basement.
   Music will follow." Or "Thursday, at 5p.m., there will be a meeting
of the Little Mothers Club. All those wishing to become Little Mothers,
please meet the pastor in his study." Or "This afternoon there will be
        a meeting in the south and north ends of the church. Children

will be baptized at both ends." Anyway . . . my Uncle Jim once said,
   "Hamsters are good for nothing but making jellybeans," and though
my dogs (twenty-two pounds total for all four) make jellybeans with
the best of God's creatures, they snuggle in the crook of my arm and lick
        me like I'm made of cotton candy, which helps when I feel like

going into the desert and climbing a pole to sit silently upon for twenty-
  eight years until someone calls me a saint. That or the world explodes
in a nuclear WHOOSH which rights every wrong, such as the myth
of Davy Crockett, who in reality was a drunk who left his wife
      and children, and was a "scout" who avoided going into battle

against the Indians by hiring a substitute, and as a congressman,
  he had one of the worst absentee records in history. Despite
the Walt Disneyification of that story, it still doesn't warrant
worldwide destruction, at least not as much the fact that *Star Trek*'s
      prime time rating was never higher than #52, and Spock's

Vulcan nerve pinch was an accident – Spock was supposed to sneak
  up behind a character and whack him on the head with a gun, but
Nimoy said a Vulcan wouldn't be so crude, so he made up the legendary
maneuver on the spot. Moving along . . . a writer friend of mine sent
      a first novel to that critic friend of mine who also is a contributing

editor to a semi-major publishing house. The book was called *The Stink
  of the Criminally Insane*, and was predicated on a crime-solving
super sleuth who relied foremost on his olfactory senses. All this was
based on a "scientific" study my writer friend did on scents. (F.Y.I. –
      according to his findings, the odors that most arouse a woman

sexually are lavender, cucumbers, baby powder, pumpkin pie, and Good
  & Plenty candy.) The book was given a form rejection, which my
writer friend tore up and fed to his dog while explaining to me on
the phone that it takes twelve ears of corn to make a tablespoon of corn
      oil, interspersed with comments about he'd like to roast my critic

friend over a pit of slag lava. "Good God, really?" I said, meaning the
   corn oil. "Damn straight," he said, meaning, I now suspect, the slag lava.
And as I hang up and go for a beer in the fridge, fed up at last, my dogs
whine for more twenty-dollar-a-bag dog food and I see the note my wife
         taped to the fridge. **Four Terms Coined by** *Star Trek*. (1) Warp drive

(2) Mind meld (3) Phaser (4) Dilithium crystals. Then I get that beer,
   and I feed those dogs their Kibbles 'n Chunks with Cheese, and I think
of my critic friend being roasted alive slowly, and I look at myself
in the mirror, saying "So?" as if I'm not a stranger and the world's
         not a TV show, and storm clouds aren't ready to rain down Clorox

on the fire-anthill of my life.

Mr. Bertel Poem #3,
or Smart-ass-ology 101

Dustin Bertel, a.k.a. "Bertie from Room 30," was originally the shop
   teacher, but cutbacks made him my seventh grade science teacher, then
   later, my English teacher, where our first project was writing letters to
         our elected representative of Illinois, Sen. Paul Simon. The purpose
of the exercise: to demonstrate that our opinions matter. To this date,

none of those letters received a response. We didn't hate Bertie, not really,
   but it was me who slapped bumper stickers onto his brown Plymouth Duster
   one night: "So many cats . . . so few recipes!" and "Don't piss me off!
         I'm running out of places to hide the bodies." I admit that he had a sense
of humor about being forced into a roomful of teenage freak shows,

but all bets were off when he said one afternoon that, "A narcissist
   is someone better looking than you are." He adored jazz, often playing
   Coltrane tapes in the background while we read poetry he assigned, usually
         frou-frou stuff like melancholy bouts of madness and leaves that turn
red and golden then ease to the ground on their own quick wings. When

we switched out his Satchmo cassette for Van Halen, he erupted, flinging
   himself onto his desk and hooting like a barn owl. The next day, we had
   Mrs. Chow instead, who didn't speak English well but read us real-life
         headlines from a joke book all period. "Body Search Reveals $4,000
in Crack." "April Slated as Child Abuse Month." "County Wants Money

for Taking Dump." Time is the great equalizer, my father told me,
   and he's right. Being a teacher now, I understand Bertie's pain, having
   recently received essays with lines such as: "One of the causes of the
         Revolutionary War was the English put tacks in their tea," and
"Writing at the same time as Shakespeare was Miguel Cervantes. He wrote

Donkey Hote. The next great author was John Milton. Milton wrote *Paradise Lost*.
Then his wife died and he wrote *Paradise Regained*." After a long day
of teaching, I sip Sahara martinis and listen to Maynard Ferguson wail
old Charlie Parker tunes. The night softens into a blouse of dark,
and I think often of Bertie, how he had the brown eyes of a good-hearted

beagle and told us that it was through the imagination that we twist over
the wet rocks of the world, an idea I only remember now as the
geese are slanting south again. Bertie returned after the Coltrane
thing, quieter perhaps, but game enough to reroute our interest
by telling us, "Tears are made up of almost the same ingredients as urine"

and "In Yukon, Oklahoma, it is illegal for a patient to pull a dentist's
tooth." Still, we poured yellow food dye in his classroom humidifier
and called him Dirty Bertie when he started dating the hot-mama
lady janitor. Just today, though, I found an entire banana
stuffed in my Blazer's tailpipe, and a bumper sticker on the windshield.

"As long as there are tests, there will be prayer in public schools."
My wife thinks it's funny. My father, knowing the rap sheet of my juvenile
years, says it's karma. But in the brisk and shallow restlessness of mid-
autumn, I come to terms with the weed-choked shore of my life:
if Bertie did not exist, it would be necessary to invent him.

Britney at the Tattoo-Removal Parlor
at Age Thirty-Five

A little girl in church who's been shushed
for whispering in the silence between psalms,
she fidgets as a bearded man snaps on plastic gloves
then administers the numbing potion, oozing red
liquid the color of a once-worn catsuit that taught
her thighs to sweat worse than her guardian angel.
Justin was here, it says in a swoop of green cursive
over her *gluteus maximus,* an impulsive act
after drinking appletinis in St. Thomas.
And she almost realizes the irony of it,
how the twenty-something doctor hunkering
over her bared ass doesn't know Justin
was the Curly-haired Wonder nor does he much care
about the ex-'N sync-er's Icarus-tumble from fame.
Her stomach aches when she's told to stoop over
further, those seven painful post-pregnancy tucks
giving thanks to her navel-driven career, each throb
a striving, a search for words as the heyday is over,
the botox unable to flatten crow's feet, and her thighs
no longer knife-edged but swollen like a hibiscus blossom.
As the pain comes in waves, she imagines herself at forty,
alone at a table, smearing honey on toast, her life
a much smaller cloud of possibilities, a cumulous mass
that is threatening rain. And with every prick, each needle-
quick stab, she's relearning how eternity is doled

        out one second, one ex-fan, at a time.

Without Bert, Ernie Lost in Purgatory

Having slipped on a dew-wet log,
Ernie tumbles headfirst into a chute
where he remains lodged between
rocks pressing hard into his balding scalp.
His strings lie torn and ragged –
no one's around to tug them, anyway.
A hatch of mosquitoes works at his legs,
his soft melon belly. Through tears,
he considers prayer, asking Big Bird
to bestow blessedness, divine intervention
upon his twisted body, but his voice
is the noise of a treefrog, incomprehensible
inside the dark dirt throat.
With philosophic calm, the clouds release
rain, each pinprick of water a millionth
of a fraction harder, faster. As the tube
begins to fill, becoming a watery casket,
Ernie thinks one last time of Bert, imagining
his chiffon friend cleaning a hunting rifle,
oiling the cold wooden stock, then testing
the weight of the bullet to put out his life.

Britney Must Die,

or

A Sonnet from the Lips of the Milwaukee Pyromaniac
Who Once Was a Music Critic But Heard Britney's
*". . . Baby One More Time \ (You Drive Me) Crazy \ I'm A Slave 4 U \ Toxic *
Oops! . . . I Did It Again \ Stronger \ Everytime"
Chris Cox Megamix and Had a Complete Breakdown

Nothing burns better than leather skivvies,
except perhaps a red lace thong, jeans with
the rear slashed and diced, Freddy Krueger-like.
Douse that bleached hair in gasoline, fill her
peek-a-boo navel with napalm jelly.
Round up Christina, Jessica, J. Lo,
those fellow witches, as the fuse is lit
to the wooden throne Britney's tied upon.

Perhaps she won't burn, perhaps her pact with
Satan's lawyers taught her to quench all flames
into the sparks from which they came. But I
say let's try: rub two sticks together, light
the blowtorch. Wreathed now in flame, her body's
still a siren song, a shriek of dark magic.

Yellow Narcissus

It's not easy being yellow
as a daffodil's skull
in a Technicolor world
that's barely 2-D and every
horizon is populated
with deserted monorails tracks
and reactor runoff pools.
In his basement, where
he confides to himself
in dark wink of cellar
gloom, he scrutinizes
his body, supervising
the health of every cell.
Self-imposed sterilization
is always an option – who
wants to pass on misfortune?
There is a nub in the crotch
of his arm, an omnipresent
pupiled eye in which he
can see himself looking
down as he gazes back up,
a real trick of optic nerve
and tissue. Some things
are best not to share, even
when your skin is glorious,
golden like the fuzz on
Perseus' chin as he arrows
through clouds, laughing,
defying prisms, nuclear physics,
the wrong side of a possessive.

Five Failed Movie Projects

Golden Hoof

Spears is shipwrecked on a deserted island and falls in love with a unicorn that's entirely a figment of her own imagination.

One Million Carats

A cop (one of the Baldwins) on leave for drinking and harassing suspects is trapped in a diamond mine with Spears during a terrorist takeover.

Emperors and Eskimos

Spears, a photojournalist on assignment for *National Geographic* in Alaska, falls in love with Nanook of the North's great grandson.

Temptation

Spears is a blonde Jesus in a cross-gender, modern-day interpretation of the Bible story. Includes a slow-motion close-up of Spears sucking a lemon-yellow lollipop.

Thirty to Life

A shampoo heiress, Spears is on trial for the decapitation of her boy-toy husband who was cheating on her with the neighbor's Latina laundrywoman. But she didn't do it; a random serial killer from Scranton did.

Bubbles Speaks

Some days I'm all banana cream pie.
Others, I fling feces down the water slide
at Neverland. It's a chimpanzee-eat-
chimpanzee world, my mother once said.
My father? He told me not to fill up
on lettuce spines. Most Saturdays, I stick
my shades on, wear my leather coat and pants,
and go see Uma Thurman movie premieres
at the multiplex where I nibble the honey-
covered termites tucked carefully under my lip.

I like how movie dark arrives the way
a house darkens, when a bedroom fills quietly
with evening. Since "Beat It," I've had
my own two-story bedroom with platinum toilet
and walk-in closet. I ate most of the buttons
off my sport coats. The Rembrandt, though,
gave me gas. I've been told I'm an A-list
monkey with B-list taste, whatever the hell that means.

Lately, M-Jack's llama has been stalking me,
jealous of my celebrity perhaps, grinding itself
in coarse dirt and taking spit potshots.
One night, while the moonlight eases upon
the ocean of waxed hardwood covering the barn,
I'll sneak up and whack that stupid animal
in the skull with a brick, watching the last steamy
exhalations plume from her lips as I revel
in the intricacy of opposable thumbs.

Truthfully, Michael and I are on the outs since I kissed
another chimp center stage on the 2003 MTV
Video Music Awards, the bony shelves of our foreheads

clacking together as her nostril hair poked at my eye,
and my tongue tested the tunnel of her mouth.

I miss the spotlight. I miss the cue cards, the grip
following me with banana milkshakes, Swisher Sweets.
I'm not a bad chimp – I'm just misunderstood.
Instead of sending in Dr. Phil, give me back
my Lake Geneva condo and three-man camera team
to film some of my binge shopping at PETsMART.
I'm not a bad chimp – I just gotta get mine,
Mont Blanc held like a knife to my throat or not.

So I Walk Into this Bar and there's the Pope,
Jacques Derrida, and Macaulay Culkin . . .

The last thing Derrida said that I understood was, *Critical theories*
  are not like tablets of stone, unaffected by the passage of time.
  This was during a lecture at NYU years back, but like slamming
    a beer right after a vodka martini, he chased it with,
  In the end, no theory can totally transcend its ideological prehistory,
    especially with appreciation to the profound implications

for political, moral, and metaphysical commitments. I remember looking
  meaningfully into my plastic cup of Diet Pepsi, thinking, *Ice cubes*
  are not like tablets of stone, unaffected by the passage of soda pop into
    my mouth. Years before this, I had a similar intellectual crisis
  on the set of *Home Alone* which filmed in Chicago in 1989.
    In a time crunch, some yahoos in sharkskin suits handed

out cash at my high school for a bunch of us to be extras. Dr. Trimbourne,
  the anorexic orchestra teacher with the Hitler moustache,
  asked why we deserved to be paid and wasn't that illegal
    and all, but the suits said, "We want these kids.
  They look real." And so for four days, we played hooky and hung
    out on the set. When the kid hired to play the Little Nero's

Pizza Delivery guy got the DTs (rumor was he'd been drinking since
  back in the day with Drew Barrymore and the *E.T.* crowd), I got
  the part by virtue of having driven for Domino's pizza for two
    days. This was during the 30-minutes-or-your-pizza-is-free
  campaign and I had five tickets before Mom's orange Chevy Caprice
    station wagon was impounded. None of the other kids had

driven pizzas, so I got to slam a car into that cast iron jockey in front
of the house, then stand around with Joe Pesci in his cop suit,
saying things like, "Someone owes me a hundred twenty-two
fifty," and "Nice tip, thanks a lot." Macaulay Culkin
had his own trailer that by contract stipulation was one foot,
one inch wide and longer than any other actor's trailer

on the lot. The other actors hated him, especially the kid who played
Fuller, because he really did have a bed-wetting problem and
all that kidding around onstage was killing his confidence
and one day, Culkin ran his drippy rubber sheets up
a flagpole and had the sound guys play "Taps," which made
Fuller pound him with a fat red wiffle ball bat. I'd love

to have seen Derrida try to question that cause and effect paradigm,
the presence and absence of urine, exposing the bias of the tacit
assumptions on which this particular example of Western
metaphysics rested. I imagine it'd begin with the center
of the event, the rubberness of the sheets, the wetnessness
of wetness. But since everything in deconstruction

is provisional and the whole key is to carry on like nothing is inappropriate
. . . Culkin refused to come out of his trailer after what privately
became known as The Wiffle Bat Incident, and no one could get
past the heavy-duty Hollywood security locks on his door,
even when an off-duty fireman was brought in with a box
of tools. During the two-day standoff, I remembered reading

about the Popemobile, how when an assassin sights a sniper rifle down
     on God's earthly mouthpiece he'll be thwarted by titanium
alloy shielding and triple-thick shatter-proof, bullet-proof,
          fire-proof glass. If I had as much stress as the Pope had to,
     I'd pull a Macaulay Culkin and hide in my car drinking Diet Pepsi
          and just watching *Family Feud* until my eyes bled,

and maybe that's what Culkin was doing, that or pondering the possibility
     that he, Macaulay Culkin, was indeed the Transcendental
Signified, the ultimate source of meaning. I spent those days
          practicing my quick-draw with Joe Pesci's fake cop pistol
     and shooting craps with Old Man Marley, the South Bend Shovel
          Slayer who had, in real life, done a nickel in Joliet

for some mail fraud. When Culkin finally came out, the real pizza kid
     was back on the sauce and ready to go, so I got booted, stuck with
my high school buddies as extras in O'Hare who get knocked
          out of the way as the MacAllisters hurried to their Paris
     flight (I'm the one with the red ski hat and galoshes, sadly nothing
          more than a red blur in the final cut). In true Derrida-

fashion, the binary opposition of my potential movie star fame
     came into play soon after – the complete anonymity of high
school, where for movie-hooky detention, a dozen of us had
          to march the muddy shores of the Palatine reservoir
     an hour each day for two weeks, burrs in socks, beggar ticks
          burrowing deep, and with each faltering step we wheezed

that infamous line from *Angels with Filthy Souls*, our *Home Alone* mantra,
     our last link to four days of escape: *Keep the change, you filthy animals.*

Errata

On page 35, replace every usage of "Troy Sr." with "scatterbrained loser who is marked for death." This was a regrettable printing error. The rolling sound you hear comes, indeed, from heads.

In general, it would be best to plain ignore the poems about the Canadian Tourist Bureau unless you too have had a negative experience in Vancouver with streetcart vendor unagi or a pot-smoking hemophiliac who claimed to sell discount ferry tickets to Victoria Island. If you know or are related to either man, I recommend page 24. Pay particular attention to the associative qualities of the wood ducks as they experience an unexpected encounter with .00 buckshot.

Also, it's true that too few of the poems in this collection begin with a metaphor. *Mea culpa*. Hence, I offer: You are the jackal-headed god of the underworld.

If that metaphor is not to your liking, use the following figurations in succession, or reorder as needed: (1) Morning surprises us like a wink in closet-dark. (2) A bohemian waxwing jabbers like nobody's business. (3) I'd kiss a million horses before I touch your chocolate blueberry pie.

Honestly, no one does the Dirty Dog or Watusi anymore, despite what is tangentially suggested in the poem on dancing on page 51. Also, the poet's father no longer wears a particularly small velour hat, nor did dogs run amuck in Nettles Park in Clemson, South Carolina during a Jaycee weenie roast in '04. These were inventions of the poet that now seem happy as headstones. Apologies all around.

Finally, the following had been editorially excised from the text of various poems. After substantial time in the poet's pocket, they have been re-assembled here to be applied liberally back to the text – season to taste – or to spice up other texts of your own choosing.

scuff through the underbrush

she was an advertisement for Zoloft

I'll have to forget her to know she's gone

bad as bear droppings

bat an eyelash @ a kiss thrown by
Tiger Woods from the third teebox

amber-colored light flooding down. . .

these poems doggishly chew the bed ruffle,
wet the rugs, and snuffle post holes –
can I whack their snouts with rolled-up newspaper?

Errata addendum:

Please ignore the previous errata. It was to be a postscript to a different book entirely and its appearance here is a regrettable printing error. Thank you, and apologies *ad nauseam*.

Notes

The Shar Jackson epigraph comes from an April 2004 edition of *USA Today*.

Britney's poem, excerpted in epigraph two, can easily be found in its entirety by using an Internet search engine.

"Counter-Terrorist Barbie": *El Guerrero Cobre* (Spanish) – "the copper warrior"; this poem is for Denise Duhamel.

"Benevolence: A Love Story Between Britney Spears and Animal from the Muppets" is for David Lehman.

The entire text of "Simon Says" comes from the words of Simon Cowell (b. 1959), the English record producer and caustic judge on Britain's *Pop Idol* and the U.S.'s *American Idol*.

"Kong Speaks: A Three-Part Nocturne" is for William Trowbridge. This poem is in response to his inspiring poetry collection, *The Complete Book of Kong*.

"Sin Poem #5 – The Avarice Poem, or After Reading Martín Espada's *Imagine the Angels of Bread*, I Want to Kick His Ass": *casa* (Spanish) – "home"; *como un buitre* (Spanish) – "like a vulture"; *loco* (Spanish) – "crazy"; *Buena Suerte* (Spanish) – "good luck"; *¡Viva la poesía! ¡Viva Martín!* (Spanish) – "Long live poetry! Long live Martín!"

The inspiration for "Bubbles Speaks" comes largely from the following article excerpt (www.popdirt, 10/25/03): Sheryl Crow has revealed Michael Jackson used to torture his chimp, Bubbles. Sheryl said, "He was big enough to be pretty dangerous. Mike used to calm him down by shoving a ballpoint in his chest."

"So I Walk Into This Bar and There's the Pope, Jacques Derrida, and Macaulay Culkin . . ." is for Miles Watson.